STRATEGIC STORYTELLING

Crafting Narratives for Marketing Success

VIOLET WAKEFIELD

Copyright © 2024 by Violet Wakefield

All rights reserved. No part of this book may be reproduced, stored in a retrieval system, or transmitted, in any form or by any means, electronic, mechanical, photocopying, recording, or otherwise, without the prior written permission of the author, except in the case of brief quotations embodied in critical reviews and certain other noncommercial uses permitted by copyright law.

TABLE OF CONTENT

INTRODUCTION 5

CHAPTER 1: THE POWER OF NARRATIVE: UNDERSTANDING STORYTELLING IN MARKETING .. 7

- The Psychology of Storytelling: How Narratives Influence Consumer Behavior 9

- Storytelling in the Digital Age: Adapting Traditional Narratives to Modern Platforms 12

- Story Structures and Archetypes: Crafting Compelling Narratives for Different Audiences 17

CHAPTER 2: CRAFTING YOUR BRAND STORY: DEVELOPING A COMPELLING NARRATIVE IDENTITY 21

- Defining Your Brand's Narrative Essence: Core Values and Mission Statements 23

- Creating a Character: Personifying Your Brand Through Storytelling 28

- Storytelling Workshops: Collaborative Approaches to Developing Brand Narratives 33

CHAPTER 3: EMOTIONAL ENGAGEMENT: LEVERAGING STORYTELLING TO CONNECT WITH YOUR AUDIENCE 40

- Emotional Storytelling Techniques: Eliciting Emotions for Brand Engagement 42

- Empathy and Authenticity: Building Trust Through Transparent Narratives 49

- Storytelling for Social Impact: Connecting with Customers on a Deeper Level 55

CHAPTER 4: STORYTELLING ACROSS CHANNELS: STRATEGIES FOR EFFECTIVE MULTICHANNEL NARRATIVES 62

- Integrated Marketing Communications: Aligning Narratives Across Channels 64

- Storytelling in Social Media: Leveraging Visual and Interactive Elements 70

- Omnichannel Storytelling: Creating Seamless Experiences Across Touchpoints 77

CHAPTER 5: MEASURING SUCCESS: METRICS AND ANALYSIS FOR STORYTELLING IMPACT 86

- Key Performance Indicators (KPIs) for Storytelling: Metrics That Matter 88

- Data Analytics and Storytelling: Using Insights to Refine Narrative Strategies 96

- ROI of Storytelling: Evaluating the Business Impact of Narrative-driven Marketing 103

CONCLUSION 111

INTRODUCTION

"Strategic Storytelling: Crafting Narratives for Marketing Success" invites you into a realm where the power of narrative transforms marketing from a mere transactional tool to an immersive journey of connection and persuasion. In a digital age inundated with information, storytelling stands as the beacon of engagement, weaving emotional resonance into the fabric of brands. This book is a roadmap for marketers, entrepreneurs, and storytellers alike, navigating the intricate landscape of strategic storytelling.

Through these pages, you'll discover the alchemy of narrative, blending data-driven insights with the art of captivating storytelling. We delve into the psychology of storytelling, understanding how narratives shape perceptions, evoke emotions, and drive action. Each chapter is a tapestry of practical strategies, case studies, and actionable techniques, equipping you to craft narratives that resonate deeply with your audience.

From defining your brand's narrative identity to leveraging storytelling across diverse marketing channels, this book empowers you to harness the full potential of storytelling in today's competitive market. Whether you're building brand loyalty, launching a product, or engaging your audience, Strategic Storytelling is your guide to crafting narratives that not only captivate but also drive tangible results in the ever-evolving landscape of modern marketing.

CHAPTER 1: THE POWER OF NARRATIVE: UNDERSTANDING STORYTELLING IN MARKETING

In Chapter 1 of "Strategic Storytelling: Crafting Narratives for Marketing Success," titled "The Power of Narrative: Understanding Storytelling in Marketing," we embark on a journey into the heart of storytelling's transformative influence on modern marketing strategies. In today's dynamic and digitally-driven landscape, storytelling has emerged as a paramount force, reshaping how brands connect with their audiences and drive meaningful engagement.

This chapter serves as a foundational exploration, delving deep into the psychology, mechanics, and strategic applications of narrative in marketing. We unravel the intricate threads of storytelling's power, examining how narratives evoke emotions, shape perceptions, and foster enduring connections with consumers. Through a blend of theory and practical insights, we uncover the essence of storytelling as a catalyst for brand differentiation and customer loyalty.

As we navigate through this chapter, we'll unravel the storytelling techniques that captivate audiences across diverse platforms, from traditional media to digital realms. By understanding the core principles of effective storytelling, marketers and entrepreneurs gain invaluable tools to craft compelling narratives that resonate with authenticity and impact. Join me as we unravel the art and science behind harnessing the power of narrative to unlock marketing success.

The Psychology of Storytelling: How Narratives Influence Consumer Behavior

The psychology of storytelling delves into the intricate ways narratives shape human cognition, emotions, and behavior. Understanding this psychology is crucial for marketers seeking to leverage storytelling as a powerful tool to influence consumer behavior. Here's a comprehensive discussion on how narratives influence consumer behavior:

1. **Emotional Impact**: Narratives have a profound impact on emotions. Stories have the ability to evoke a wide range of emotions, from joy and excitement to sadness and empathy. When consumers emotionally connect with a brand's story, they are more likely to develop a positive attitude

towards the brand, leading to increased loyalty and engagement.

2. **Cognitive Processing:** Stories are processed differently in the brain compared to facts and data. When people hear a story, multiple areas of their brain are activated, including those responsible for language processing, sensory experiences, and emotions. This multisensory activation makes stories more memorable and persuasive than straightforward information.

3. **Engagement and Attention:** Storytelling captures attention and sustains engagement. Compared to traditional advertising that often gets tuned out, narratives draw people in and keep them interested. This increased engagement can lead to higher retention of brand messages and increased willingness to act on those messages.

4. **Identification and Relatability:** Effective storytelling allows consumers to see themselves in the narrative. When people can relate to the characters or situations in a story, they are more

likely to internalize the message and feel a personal connection with the brand. This sense of identification can drive purchase decisions and brand loyalty.

5. **Behavioral Influence:** Narratives can influence consumer behavior by shaping perceptions, preferences, and decision-making processes. Stories that highlight the benefits of a product or service in a relatable context can lead to increased desire and motivation to make a purchase.

6. **Story Arcs and Resonance:** The structure of a story, including its beginning, middle, and end, plays a crucial role in how it impacts consumer behavior. Well-crafted story arcs that build tension, create anticipation, and offer resolution can leave a lasting impression on consumers, influencing their attitudes and actions.

7. **Social Influence:** Stories have a social dimension that can influence behavior through social proof, peer influence, and cultural resonance. When a story aligns with societal values, norms, or trends, it

can gain traction and influence a wider audience, driving collective behaviors and preferences.

In summary, the psychology of storytelling reveals that narratives are not just entertainment; they are powerful tools for shaping beliefs, attitudes, and behaviors. Marketers who understand how storytelling influences consumer psychology can craft compelling narratives that resonate deeply with their target audience, driving meaningful engagement and driving desired actions.

- Storytelling in the Digital Age: Adapting Traditional Narratives to Modern Platforms

Storytelling in the Digital Age involves adapting traditional narrative techniques to suit the unique characteristics and demands of modern digital platforms. This adaptation is essential for marketers and content creators to effectively engage with audiences who consume information in diverse ways across various digital channels. Let's comprehensively discuss the key aspects of storytelling in the digital age:

1. **Multimedia Storytelling:** Digital platforms offer a plethora of multimedia formats, including videos, images, infographics, animations, and interactive content. Effective storytelling in the digital age leverages these multimedia elements to create immersive experiences that captivate and engage audiences. By combining visuals, audio, and interactive elements, storytellers can convey complex narratives in compelling ways that resonate with modern audiences.

2. **Interactive and User-Generated Content:** Digital storytelling goes beyond one-way communication. It involves creating opportunities for interaction and engagement through user-generated content, polls, quizzes, surveys, and interactive storytelling experiences. Engaging audiences in participatory storytelling not only

fosters a sense of belonging and ownership but also enhances brand loyalty and advocacy.

3. Personalization and Customization: Digital platforms allow for personalized storytelling experiences based on user preferences, behaviors, and demographics. Marketers can leverage data analytics and automation tools to deliver tailored content that speaks directly to individual audience members. Personalized storytelling enhances relevance, increases engagement, and drives conversion rates by delivering the right message to the right person at the right time.

4. Real-Time Storytelling: The real-time nature of digital platforms enables brands to engage in timely and relevant storytelling. Marketers can capitalize on trending topics, current events, and social conversations to create authentic and impactful narratives that resonate with audiences in the moment. Real-time storytelling fosters brand agility, responsiveness, and cultural relevance, positioning brands as dynamic and connected entities.

5. **Cross-Platform Storytelling:** Digital storytelling is not confined to a single platform but spans across multiple channels and devices. Marketers must adapt their narratives for various digital platforms such as social media, websites, blogs, podcasts, streaming services, and mobile apps. Consistent storytelling across platforms ensures brand coherence, maximizes reach, and facilitates seamless user experiences.

6. **Data-Driven Storytelling:** In the digital age, storytelling is increasingly informed by data insights and analytics. Marketers can analyze audience behavior, engagement metrics, and performance indicators to optimize storytelling strategies, refine content delivery, and measure impact. Data-driven storytelling empowers brands to make informed decisions, iterate on content strategies, and drive continuous improvement in storytelling effectiveness.

7. **Transmedia Storytelling:** Transmedia storytelling involves telling a cohesive narrative across multiple media platforms and formats. It

encourages audience participation, exploration, and immersion in a story world that extends beyond traditional boundaries. Transmedia storytelling allows for deeper engagement, fan interaction, and the creation of expansive narrative universes that captivate and inspire audiences across digital ecosystems.

In conclusion, storytelling in the digital age is about embracing innovation, interactivity, personalization, and data-driven insights to create compelling narratives that resonate with modern audiences. By adapting traditional storytelling principles to the dynamic landscape of digital platforms, marketers can leverage the full potential of digital storytelling to connect, engage, and inspire action.

- Story Structures and Archetypes: Crafting Compelling Narratives for Different Audiences

Story structures and archetypes play a crucial role in crafting compelling narratives for different audiences. These elements provide a framework that resonates with human psychology and cultural storytelling conventions, making stories more relatable, impactful, and memorable. Let's comprehensively discuss how story structures and archetypes contribute to crafting compelling narratives for diverse audiences:

1. **Story Structures:**

   - Linear Narrative: This traditional structure follows a chronological sequence of events, starting from exposition, rising action, climax, falling action, and resolution. Linear narratives are easy to follow and are commonly used in storytelling across various genres.

- **Nonlinear Narrative:** In contrast to linear narratives, nonlinear structures employ flashbacks, flash-forwards, and parallel storylines. Nonlinear storytelling adds complexity, suspense, and depth to narratives, keeping audiences engaged and intrigued.

- **Episodic Structure:** Episodic storytelling divides a narrative into distinct episodes or chapters, each with its own mini-arc and resolution. Episodic structures are common in serialized content such as TV series, webisodes, and episodic podcasts.

- **Circular Narrative:** Circular narratives loop back to the beginning, creating a sense of closure or cyclical themes. This structure is often used to convey themes of repetition, transformation, or eternal cycles.

2. **Archetypes:**

- **Hero's Journey:** The hero's journey archetype follows a protagonist who embarks on a transformative quest, facing challenges, allies, enemies, and ultimately undergoing personal growth and achieving a goal. This archetype resonates with universal themes of self-discovery, courage, and resilience.

  - **Villain vs. Hero:** The conflict between a hero and a villain is a classic archetype that drives narratives across genres. It embodies themes of good vs. evil, justice vs. injustice, and the hero's journey to overcome adversity.

  - **The Mentor:** The mentor archetype represents a wise and guiding figure who imparts knowledge, wisdom, and support to the protagonist. Mentors play a crucial role in character development and narrative progression.

  - **The Everyman:** The everyman archetype represents an ordinary person thrust into extraordinary circumstances. Everyman characters are relatable to audiences as they navigate challenges, make choices, and undergo personal growth.

- **The Rebel:** Rebels challenge authority, norms, and conventions, embodying themes of rebellion, independence, and change. The rebel archetype appeals to audiences seeking stories of defiance, revolution, and social transformation.

Crafting compelling narratives for different audiences involves understanding which story structures and archetypes resonate with their preferences, values, and aspirations. By combining these elements creatively, storytellers can create immersive and impactful narratives that captivate, inspire, and resonate with diverse audiences across cultures and demographics.

CHAPTER 2: CRAFTING YOUR BRAND STORY: DEVELOPING A COMPELLING NARRATIVE IDENTITY

In Chapter 2 of "Strategic Storytelling: Crafting Narratives for Marketing Success," titled "Crafting Your Brand Story: Developing a Compelling Narrative Identity," we delve into the art and strategy of creating a narrative identity that resonates with audiences and drives brand loyalty. In today's competitive landscape, brands must go beyond product features and benefits to establish an emotional connection with consumers. This chapter is a guide to crafting a brand story that embodies your values, mission, and unique identity, positioning your brand as more than just a product or service—it becomes a compelling narrative that engages hearts and minds.

We explore the essential components of a brand story, from defining your brand's core essence to shaping its character and voice. Through a series of actionable insights, examples, and exercises, we navigate the process of developing a narrative that not only communicates what your brand does but also why it matters. Your brand story becomes a powerful tool for differentiation, fostering customer loyalty, and creating a lasting impact in the minds of your target audience.

Join me on this journey of crafting a compelling narrative identity for your brand—a narrative that captivates, inspires, and builds meaningful connections with your customers, driving success and resonance in a crowded marketplace.

- Defining Your Brand's Narrative Essence: Core Values and Mission Statements

Defining your brand's narrative essence through core values and mission statements is a foundational step in crafting a compelling brand story that resonates with your audience. This process involves articulating the fundamental beliefs, purpose, and direction of your brand, creating a cohesive narrative framework that guides all aspects of your marketing and communication strategies. Let's comprehensively discuss how defining your brand's narrative essence through core values and mission statements contributes to a strong brand identity:

1. **Core Values:**

   - **Definition:** Core values represent the guiding principles and beliefs that define your brand's identity and culture. They reflect what your brand stands for, its ethical standards, and the behaviors it upholds.

- **Purpose:** Identifying and articulating core values helps clarify your brand's purpose and differentiation in the market. Core values serve as a compass for decision-making, guiding actions, initiatives, and relationships both internally and externally.

- **Alignment:** Core values align stakeholders, employees, and customers around shared beliefs and expectations. They foster a sense of unity, trust, and authenticity, reinforcing brand loyalty and advocacy.

- **Examples:** Common core values include integrity, innovation, sustainability, diversity, transparency, customer-centricity, and social responsibility. These values should be authentic, meaningful, and actionable, reflecting the essence of your brand.

2. Mission Statement:

- **Definition:** A mission statement succinctly articulates your brand's purpose, goals, and primary objectives. It communicates why your brand exists, what it aims to achieve, and how it intends to make a positive impact.

- **Clarity and Focus:** A well-crafted mission statement provides clarity and focus, aligning stakeholders and resources towards common goals. It serves as a rallying cry that inspires and motivates employees, customers, and partners.

- **Differentiation:** Your mission statement should highlight what sets your brand apart from competitors and how you deliver unique value to your target audience. It encapsulates your brand's promise and commitment to fulfilling customer needs and aspirations.

- **Adaptability:** While mission statements are enduring, they should also be adaptable to evolving market trends, consumer preferences, and industry dynamics. A flexible mission statement allows for innovation, growth, and strategic pivots without compromising core values.

- **Examples:** Examples of impactful mission statements include Nike's "To bring inspiration and innovation to every athlete in the world" and Google's "To organize the world's information and make it universally accessible and useful." These statements are concise, aspirational, and reflective of the brand's core purpose and impact.

3. **Integration into Brand Storytelling:**

- **Narrative Alignment:** Core values and mission statements form the backbone of your brand's narrative identity. They should be seamlessly integrated into your brand story, messaging, content, and brand experiences.

- **Emotional Connection:** Communicating core values and mission through storytelling fosters emotional connections with your audience. Stories that exemplify your values and mission resonate deeply, creating memorable brand experiences and fostering brand loyalty.

- **Consistency and Authenticity:** Consistently reinforcing core values and mission in all brand touchpoints reinforces authenticity and trust. It builds a cohesive brand identity that customers can relate to and advocate for.

- **Evolution:** As your brand evolves, periodically review and refine your core values and mission statement to ensure they remain relevant, aspirational, and reflective of your brand's journey and impact.

In summary, defining your brand's narrative essence through core values and mission statements is essential for creating a strong brand identity, fostering customer loyalty, and driving long-term success. By aligning beliefs, purpose, and actions, your brand story becomes a powerful tool for differentiation, engagement, and meaningful connections with your target audience.

- Creating a Character: Personifying Your Brand Through Storytelling

Creating a character to personify your brand through storytelling is a powerful strategy that humanizes your brand, fosters emotional connections with your audience, and makes your brand more relatable and memorable. This approach involves developing a distinct persona, complete with traits, values, and a backstory, to embody the essence of your brand in a way that resonates with customers. Let's comprehensively discuss the process and impact of creating a character to personify your brand through storytelling:

1. **Defining Brand Persona:**

   - **Character Traits:** Identify key traits and characteristics that define your brand's personality. These traits should align with your brand's core values, mission, and positioning in the market. For example, is your brand adventurous, trustworthy, innovative, empathetic, or playful?

   - Visual Identity: Create a visual representation of your brand persona, including logos, colors, typography, and imagery. Visual elements should reflect the personality and values of your character, reinforcing brand recognition and identity.

   - Voice and Tone: Develop a consistent voice and tone for your brand persona across communication channels. Consider the language style, vocabulary, and messaging approach that best reflects your character's personality and resonates with your target audience.

2. **Crafting a Backstory:**

   - Origin Story: Develop an engaging backstory that explains how your brand came to be, its journey, challenges faced, and successes achieved. A compelling origin story adds depth and authenticity to your brand persona, making it more relatable and human.

- **Character Arc:** Like a protagonist in a story, your brand persona should have a character arc that evolves over time. This evolution can reflect changes in market trends, customer feedback, and brand growth, maintaining relevance and resonance with your audience.

3. **Emotional Connection:**

- **Relatability:** A well-developed brand character allows customers to relate to your brand on a personal level. Humanizing your brand creates empathy, trust, and emotional connections that go beyond transactional relationships.

- **Storytelling Impact:** Incorporate your brand character into storytelling narratives across marketing campaigns, content creation, and brand experiences. Use storytelling techniques such as anecdotes, testimonials, and user-generated content to showcase your brand persona in action and connect with your audience's emotions.

4. **Brand Consistency:**

   - **Consistent Representation:** Ensure that your brand character is consistently represented across all touchpoints, from advertising and social media to customer service interactions and product packaging. Consistency builds brand recognition and reinforces the authenticity of your brand persona.

   - **Alignment with Values:** Your brand character should embody the values, beliefs, and mission of your brand. Any actions or decisions made by your character should align with these core principles, maintaining trust and credibility with your audience.

5. **Interactive Engagement:**

   - **Engagement Opportunities:** Create interactive experiences that allow customers to engage with your brand character. This could include interactive storytelling, gamification, virtual assistants, or social media interactions where customers can interact with your character persona.

- **User-Generated Content:** Encourage user-generated content that features interactions with your brand character. User stories, testimonials, and creative expressions can amplify the reach and impact of your brand persona, fostering community and advocacy.

6. **Adaptability and Evolution:**

- **Adapting to Audience Feedback:** Monitor audience feedback and insights to adapt and evolve your brand character as needed. Listen to customer perceptions, preferences, and expectations to ensure your character remains relevant and resonant.

- **Seasonal Campaigns and Themes:** Leverage seasonal themes, cultural events, or trending topics to incorporate your brand character into relevant campaigns and narratives. Flexibility and adaptability allow your character persona to stay dynamic and engaging.

In summary, creating a character to personify your brand through storytelling is a strategic approach that adds depth, relatability, and emotional resonance to your brand identity. By crafting a compelling character persona, developing a backstory, fostering emotional connections, maintaining brand consistency, and embracing interactive engagement, you can humanize your brand and create meaningful connections with your audience that drive brand loyalty and advocacy.

- Storytelling Workshops: Collaborative Approaches to Developing Brand Narratives

Storytelling workshops are collaborative sessions that bring together diverse stakeholders within an organization to develop and refine brand narratives. These workshops provide a structured and interactive environment for brainstorming, ideation, and creativity, fostering alignment, clarity, and engagement around the brand's storytelling strategies. Let's comprehensively discuss the process and benefits of storytelling workshops in developing brand narratives:

1. **Purpose and Objectives:**

   - **Alignment:** Storytelling workshops align stakeholders, including marketing teams, executives, creatives, and external partners, around a common understanding of the brand's narrative direction, goals, and messaging.

   - **Clarity:** Workshops clarify the brand's core values, mission, unique selling propositions (USPs), target audience personas, and competitive positioning. This clarity helps ensure consistency and coherence in storytelling across all touchpoints.

   - **Engagement:** Collaborative workshops foster active participation, creativity, and buy-in from participants, enhancing motivation, commitment, and ownership of the brand narrative development process.

2. **Key Components of Storytelling Workshops:**

- **Ideation Sessions:** Brainstorming sessions allow participants to generate ideas, themes, story angles, and content concepts that align with the brand's objectives and resonate with the target audience.

- **Persona Development:** Workshops include exercises to define and flesh out customer personas, including demographics, psychographics, pain points, aspirations, and preferred storytelling formats.

- **Story Mapping:** Participants collaboratively map out the brand's narrative journey, including key touchpoints, story arcs, messaging sequences, and emotional triggers that guide storytelling across customer journeys.

- **Character Creation:** Workshops may involve creating or refining brand characters, spokespersons, or symbolic figures that personify the brand's personality, values, and voice.

- **Content Ideation:** Participants ideate content formats, channels, and distribution strategies that maximize the impact of brand narratives, such as videos, blogs, social media campaigns, podcasts, and interactive experiences.

- **Feedback and Iteration:** Workshops include feedback loops and iteration cycles where participants review, refine, and iterate on storytelling elements based on peer feedback, expert insights, and audience testing.

3. **Benefits of Storytelling Workshops:**

- **Cross-Functional Collaboration:** Workshops break silos and encourage cross-functional collaboration, leveraging diverse perspectives, expertise, and insights from different departments and roles within the organization.

- **Creativity and Innovation:** Collaborative workshops foster creativity, innovation, and out-of-the-box thinking in developing brand narratives that stand out, inspire, and resonate with audiences.

- **Empathy and Audience Understanding:** Workshops promote empathy and a deeper understanding of the audience's needs, preferences, pain points, and aspirations, enabling brands to create more relevant and impactful stories.

- **Alignment with Brand Strategy:** Storytelling workshops ensure alignment between brand narratives and broader brand strategies, marketing objectives, brand positioning, and messaging frameworks.

- **Ownership and Commitment:** Involving stakeholders in storytelling workshops enhances their ownership, commitment, and accountability for driving the success of brand narratives, leading to more effective execution and implementation.

- **Continuous Improvement:** Workshops support continuous improvement and optimization of brand narratives through ongoing monitoring, measurement, and adaptation based on performance data, audience feedback, and market insights.

4. **Best Practices for Storytelling Workshops:**

- **Facilitation:** Skilled facilitators lead storytelling workshops, ensuring active participation, inclusion, and effective collaboration among participants.

- **Preparation:** Pre-workshop preparation, including agenda setting, participant briefings, and resource materials, helps maximize the productivity and outcomes of the workshop.

- **Post-Workshop Action Plans:** Define action plans, responsibilities, timelines, and milestones following the workshop to implement and execute the developed brand narratives effectively.

- **Feedback Mechanisms:** Incorporate feedback mechanisms and evaluation criteria to assess the impact, effectiveness, and ROI of brand narratives developed through storytelling workshops.

In summary, storytelling workshops are instrumental in developing brand narratives that resonate, inspire, and engage audiences. By fostering collaboration, creativity, alignment, empathy, and continuous improvement, these workshops empower organizations to create compelling brand stories that differentiate, connect, and drive meaningful impact in the market.

CHAPTER 3: EMOTIONAL ENGAGEMENT: LEVERAGING STORYTELLING TO CONNECT WITH YOUR AUDIENCE

In Chapter 3 of "Strategic Storytelling: Crafting Narratives for Marketing Success," titled "Emotional Engagement: Leveraging Storytelling to Connect with Your Audience," we delve into the profound impact of storytelling on creating emotional connections that resonate with audiences on a deeper level. In today's saturated and fast-paced digital landscape, capturing attention and fostering meaningful engagement requires more than just conveying information—it requires evoking emotions that inspire, empathize, and connect.

This chapter is a journey into the art and science of emotional storytelling, exploring how narratives have the power to elicit emotions, shape perceptions, and drive action. We uncover the psychology behind emotional engagement, examining how storytelling techniques such as relatability, authenticity, and empathy can transform brand-customer relationships.

Through real-world examples, best practices, and practical strategies, we navigate the strategies and tactics for leveraging storytelling to create emotional resonance with your audience. Whether it's tapping into universal emotions, crafting compelling character narratives, or weaving empathetic storytelling into your brand's DNA, this chapter equips you with the tools and insights to connect authentically and meaningfully with your audience.

Join me as we explore the transformative potential of emotional engagement through storytelling, unlocking the keys to building lasting connections, loyalty, and advocacy with your target audience.

- Emotional Storytelling Techniques: Eliciting Emotions for Brand Engagement

Emotional storytelling techniques are powerful tools for eliciting emotions and creating deep, meaningful connections with your audience. These techniques go beyond conveying information to evoke specific feelings, attitudes, and responses that resonate with your target audience. Let's comprehensively discuss the various emotional storytelling techniques and how they can be used to enhance brand engagement:

1. **Identify Emotional Triggers:**

   - **Empathy:** Empathetic storytelling puts the audience in the shoes of characters or situations, eliciting emotions such as compassion, understanding, and shared experiences. It humanizes brands and fosters connections based on empathy.

   - **Inspiration:** Inspirational stories evoke emotions like hope, motivation, and empowerment. They showcase overcoming challenges, achieving dreams, and making a positive impact, inspiring audiences to take action and believe in the brand's values.

   - **Nostalgia:** Nostalgic storytelling taps into memories, nostalgia, and sentimental feelings associated with past experiences. It creates a sense of familiarity, comfort, and emotional resonance, strengthening brand affinity and loyalty.

   - **Surprise and Delight:** Surprise storytelling involves unexpected twists, surprises, or delightful moments that evoke emotions of joy, excitement, and curiosity. It captures attention, creates memorable experiences, and leaves a lasting positive impression.

- **Fear and Urgency:** Fear-based storytelling triggers emotions like concern, urgency, and the desire for solutions. It highlights risks, challenges, or consequences, motivating audiences to take action, make changes, or seek solutions offered by the brand.

2. **Character-Centric Narratives:**

- **Relatable Characters:** Develop characters that audiences can relate to, empathize with, or aspire to be like. Humanize your brand by showcasing the struggles, triumphs, and growth of characters, creating emotional connections and building rapport.

- **Character Arcs:** Craft narratives with character arcs that involve transformation, growth, or overcoming obstacles. Audiences resonate with stories of resilience, personal development, and authenticity, strengthening brand trust and credibility.

- **Backstories:** Provide backstory elements that add depth, context, and emotional resonance to characters. Backstories reveal motivations, challenges, and aspirations, allowing audiences to connect emotionally and understand the brand's narrative journey.

3. **Visual and Sensory Storytelling:**

- **Visual Imagery:** Use visual storytelling techniques such as compelling imagery, videos, animations, and graphics to evoke emotions visually. Visual elements should complement and enhance the emotional impact of narratives.

- **Sound and Music:** Incorporate soundscapes, music, and audio effects to create emotional ambiance and enhance storytelling immersion. Music and sound cues can evoke specific emotions and enhance storytelling impact.

- **Sensory Descriptions:** Describe sensory experiences such as sights, sounds, smells, tastes, and textures to engage multiple senses and create immersive storytelling experiences. Sensory storytelling triggers emotional responses and enhances audience engagement.

4. **Story Structure and Pace:**

   - **Emotional Arcs:** Structure narratives with emotional arcs that build tension, anticipation, and emotional climaxes. Emotional arcs involve peaks and valleys of emotions, keeping audiences engaged and invested in the story's outcome.

   - **Pacing:** Control the pacing of storytelling to modulate emotional intensity. Slow pacing can build suspense and anticipation, while fast pacing can evoke excitement, urgency, and energy.

5. **Authenticity and Vulnerability:**

   - **Authenticity:** Authentic storytelling involves sharing genuine, transparent, and relatable stories that resonate with audiences' values, beliefs, and experiences. Authenticity builds trust, credibility, and emotional connection with the brand.

- **Vulnerability:** Vulnerable storytelling includes moments of vulnerability, honesty, and authenticity that humanize the brand and foster empathy. Vulnerability creates emotional openness, relatability, and authenticity in brand storytelling.

6. **Interactive and Participatory Elements:**

- **User-Generated Content:** Encourage user-generated content that shares personal stories, testimonials, and experiences related to the brand. User stories create emotional connections, build community, and amplify brand advocacy.

- **Interactive Experiences:** Create interactive storytelling experiences that allow audiences to engage, participate, and influence the narrative. Interactive elements enhance emotional engagement, immersion, and brand interaction.

7. **Call to Action and Resolution:**

- **Emotional Call to Action:** Conclude storytelling with a clear emotional call to action that aligns with the emotions evoked in the narrative. Emotional calls to action motivate audiences to take specific actions, whether it's sharing, purchasing, subscribing, or advocating for the brand.

- Resolution: Provide resolution or closure in storytelling that satisfies emotional expectations, resolves conflicts, and leaves audiences with a sense of fulfillment, empowerment, or inspiration.

In summary, emotional storytelling techniques are essential for creating compelling narratives that connect, engage, and resonate with audiences on an emotional level. By leveraging emotional triggers, character-centric narratives, visual and sensory storytelling, authentic storytelling, interactive elements, and emotional calls to action, brands can enhance brand engagement, loyalty, and advocacy through powerful storytelling experiences.

- Empathy and Authenticity: Building Trust Through Transparent Narratives

Empathy and authenticity are key pillars in building trust and fostering meaningful connections with your audience through transparent narratives. These qualities humanize your brand, create emotional resonance, and demonstrate a genuine commitment to understanding and addressing the needs, values, and experiences of your audience. Let's comprehensively discuss how empathy and authenticity contribute to trust-building through transparent narratives:

1. **Empathy in Narratives:**

   - Understanding Audience Emotions:
Empathetic storytelling involves understanding and acknowledging the emotions, struggles, aspirations,

and perspectives of your audience. It requires putting yourself in their shoes and showing genuine care and concern for their well-being.

- **Relatable Experiences:** Share stories and experiences that resonate with the lived experiences of your audience. Highlight common challenges, triumphs, and moments of vulnerability that create empathy and build rapport.

- **Emotional Connection:** Empathy creates an emotional connection with your audience by showing that you understand their feelings, validate their experiences, and are committed to addressing their needs and concerns.

- **Conflict Resolution:** Use storytelling to address conflicts, challenges, or pain points that your audience may face. Show empathy by offering solutions, support, and guidance that demonstrate your brand's commitment to helping and improving lives.

2. **Authenticity in Narratives:**

- **Transparent Communication:** Authentic storytelling involves transparent communication that is honest, genuine, and free from exaggeration or deception. It entails sharing real experiences, insights, and perspectives without hiding flaws or shortcomings.

- **Consistency with Values:** Align narratives with your brand's core values, mission, and beliefs. Authenticity shines through when your stories reflect the principles and standards that guide your brand's decisions and actions.

- **Humanize Your Brand:** Humanize your brand by showcasing the people, stories, and values behind the products or services. Authentic narratives put a face to your brand, making it relatable, trustworthy, and memorable.

- **Vulnerability and Humility:** Embrace vulnerability and humility in storytelling by acknowledging mistakes, lessons learned, and areas for improvement. Authenticity thrives when brands show humility, openness, and a willingness to listen and learn from their audience.

3. **Building Trust Through Transparency:**

- **Openness and Clarity:** Transparent narratives are clear, straightforward, and free from ambiguity or hidden agendas. They provide audiences with accurate information, context, and insights into your brand's values, processes, and decision-making.

- **Honesty and Integrity:** Demonstrate honesty and integrity in storytelling by avoiding misleading claims, exaggerated promises, or manipulative tactics. Uphold ethical standards and be transparent about your brand's practices and policies.

- **Feedback and Accountability:** Invite feedback, criticism, and suggestions from your audience, and demonstrate accountability by addressing concerns, acknowledging mistakes, and taking corrective actions. Transparency builds trust by showing that you value transparency and are committed to continuous improvement.

- **Consistency and Reliability:** Consistently deliver on your promises, commitments, and brand values. Reliability builds trust over time, reinforcing your brand's credibility and authenticity in the eyes of your audience.

4. Embodying Empathy and Authenticity in Brand Culture:

- **Internal Alignment:** Ensure internal alignment and consistency between your brand's external narratives and internal culture, values, and practices. Empathy and authenticity should be embedded in every aspect of your organization's operations and interactions.

- **Employee Advocacy:** Empower employees to embody empathy and authenticity in their interactions with customers, stakeholders, and each other. Employee advocacy strengthens trust by showcasing genuine care, empathy, and authenticity in all touchpoints.

- **Community Engagement:** Engage with your community, listen to their feedback, and demonstrate empathy and authenticity in how you respond to their needs, concerns, and contributions. Community engagement builds trust, loyalty, and advocacy among your audience.

5. **Measuring Impact and Iterating:**

 - **Feedback Analysis:** Analyze feedback, sentiment analysis, and audience responses to your narratives to gauge the impact of empathy and authenticity. Use insights to iterate, improve, and refine your storytelling strategies.

 - **Metrics of Trust:** Monitor metrics such as brand trust, customer loyalty, advocacy, and brand perception to assess the effectiveness of your transparent narratives in building trust through empathy and authenticity.

 - **Continuous Improvement:** Commit to continuous improvement by learning from successes and failures, adapting to changing audience expectations, and evolving your storytelling approach to maintain relevance and resonance.

In summary, empathy and authenticity are foundational elements in building trust through transparent narratives. By infusing empathy into your stories, showcasing authenticity in your communications, embodying transparency in your brand practices, and fostering a culture of empathy and authenticity internally and externally, you can strengthen trust, deepen connections, and create lasting impact with your audience.

- Storytelling for Social Impact: Connecting with Customers on a Deeper Level

Storytelling for social impact goes beyond traditional marketing objectives to create narratives that resonate with customers on a deeper level, inspire action, and drive positive change in society. This approach leverages storytelling techniques to address social issues, advocate for causes, and foster empathy, awareness, and engagement among audiences. Let's comprehensively discuss the strategies and impact of storytelling for social impact in connecting with customers:

1. **Identifying Social Issues:**

   - **Research and Analysis:** Identify relevant social issues, causes, or challenges that align with your brand's values, mission, and target audience interests. Conduct research, analyze trends, and engage with stakeholders to understand key issues and their impact.

   - **Prioritization:** Prioritize social issues based on their relevance, urgency, and alignment with your brand's capabilities, resources, and potential for impact. Focus on issues that resonate deeply with your audience and have the potential for meaningful change.

2. **Crafting Compelling Narratives:**

   - **Human Stories:** Share human stories and experiences that highlight the impact of social issues on individuals, communities, or the environment. Personal narratives create empathy, emotional resonance, and a sense of urgency for action.

- **Authenticity:** Maintain authenticity and transparency in storytelling by showcasing real voices, experiences, and perspectives. Avoid sensationalism or exploitation of social issues for marketing purposes.

- **Empowerment:** Empower marginalized voices, communities, and stakeholders to share their stories, advocate for change, and participate in the narrative creation process. Amplify diverse perspectives and amplify underrepresented voices.

- **Hope and Resilience:** Highlight stories of hope, resilience, and positive change that inspire audiences and showcase the potential for collective impact and solutions to social challenges.

3. **Engaging and Educating Audiences:**

- **Emotional Appeal:** Evoke emotions such as empathy, compassion, concern, and hope through storytelling. Emotional engagement creates a deeper connection with audiences and motivates them to take action or support social causes.

- **Education and Awareness:** Use storytelling to educate audiences about social issues, root causes, consequences, and potential solutions. Raise awareness, challenge stereotypes, and promote informed dialogue and understanding.

- **Call to Action:** Include a clear call to action in your storytelling that invites audiences to get involved, support initiatives, donate, volunteer, or advocate for change. Provide actionable steps and resources for engagement.

4. **Leveraging Platforms and Channels:**

- **Digital Storytelling:** Utilize digital platforms, social media, blogs, podcasts, videos, and interactive content to amplify social impact storytelling. Leverage multimedia formats to reach diverse audiences and maximize engagement.

- **Partnerships and Collaborations:** Collaborate with nonprofits, advocacy groups, influencers, and community leaders to amplify social impact narratives, reach new audiences, and mobilize support for causes.

- **User-Generated Content:** Encourage user-generated content that shares personal stories, experiences, and actions related to social impact. User stories build community, authenticity, and collective action.

- **Storytelling Events:** Organize storytelling events, workshops, webinars, or campaigns that bring together stakeholders, raise awareness, and foster dialogue and collaboration around social issues.

5. **Measuring Impact and Effectiveness:**

- **Metrics:** Define key performance indicators (KPIs) to measure the impact and effectiveness of social impact storytelling. Metrics may include engagement rates, reach, audience sentiment, conversions, donations, and advocacy actions.

- **Feedback and Evaluation:** Gather feedback from audiences, stakeholders, and partners to evaluate the impact, resonance, and relevance of social impact narratives. Use insights to iterate, improve, and refine storytelling strategies.

   - Impact Assessment: Assess the real-world impact of storytelling efforts on social change, policy advocacy, community empowerment, and overall awareness and action around social issues.

6. **Sustainability and Long-Term Commitment:**

   - Long-Term Strategy: Develop a long-term strategy and commitment to social impact storytelling that aligns with your brand's values and business objectives. Sustainability involves ongoing engagement, collaboration, and advocacy for social change.

   - Measurement of Progress: Track progress and milestones in social impact initiatives and storytelling efforts. Celebrate successes, learn from challenges, and adapt strategies to maximize impact and sustainability.

In summary, storytelling for social impact is a powerful tool for connecting with customers on a deeper level, driving engagement, and catalyzing positive change. By crafting compelling narratives, engaging and educating audiences, leveraging digital platforms and partnerships, measuring impact, and committing to long-term sustainability, brands can make a meaningful difference in addressing social issues and building a more empathetic and socially conscious society.

CHAPTER 4: STORYTELLING ACROSS CHANNELS: STRATEGIES FOR EFFECTIVE MULTICHANNEL NARRATIVES

In Chapter 4 of "Strategic Storytelling: Crafting Narratives for Marketing Success," titled "Storytelling Across Channels: Strategies for Effective Multichannel Narratives," we embark on a journey into the dynamic realm of multichannel storytelling. In today's interconnected digital landscape, reaching and engaging audiences across diverse platforms, channels, and touchpoints is essential for amplifying the impact of your brand narratives and fostering meaningful connections.

This chapter delves into the strategies, techniques, and best practices for crafting compelling narratives that seamlessly transcend traditional boundaries and resonate across multiple channels. From social media and websites to email campaigns, videos, podcasts, and beyond, we explore how to leverage each channel's unique strengths to deliver cohesive, resonant storytelling experiences.

Join me as we uncover the art and science of multichannel storytelling, discovering how to tailor narratives for different platforms, engage diverse audiences, optimize content distribution, and measure the effectiveness of your multichannel strategies. Whether you're a seasoned marketer or a budding storyteller, this chapter equips you with the insights and tools to navigate the complexities of multichannel storytelling and elevate your brand's storytelling prowess to new heights.

- Integrated Marketing Communications: Aligning Narratives Across Channels

Integrated Marketing Communications (IMC) is a strategic approach that aligns and integrates various communication channels to deliver a cohesive and unified brand message to the target audience. In the context of storytelling, IMC plays a crucial role in ensuring that narratives are consistent, complementary, and impactful across multiple channels. Let's comprehensively discuss the concept of Integrated Marketing Communications and how it aligns narratives across channels:

1. **Understanding Integrated Marketing Communications:**

   - **Holistic Approach:** IMC integrates all marketing communication channels, including advertising, public relations, direct marketing, digital marketing, social media, events, and more, into a unified and coordinated strategy.

- **Consistency:** IMC aims to ensure consistency in brand messaging, positioning, tone, and visual identity across all communication channels. Consistent storytelling builds brand recognition, credibility, and trust.

- **Synergy:** IMC leverages the synergy between different channels to amplify the impact of marketing efforts. Each channel reinforces and complements the overall brand narrative, creating a seamless and immersive experience for the audience.

2. **Key Elements of Integrated Marketing Communications for Storytelling:**

- **Brand Story:** IMC starts with a clear understanding of the brand's story, values, mission, and key messaging points. The brand story serves as the foundation for crafting narratives across channels.

- **Audience Segmentation:** IMC identifies target audience segments and tailors storytelling messages to resonate with each segment's preferences, behaviors, and communication preferences.

- **Channel Selection:** IMC selects the most appropriate channels based on audience preferences, behavior, and the nature of the message. Channels may include social media, websites, email, print media, events, influencer partnerships, and more.

- **Message Consistency:** IMC ensures that the core message, themes, and storytelling elements remain consistent across all channels. Consistency reinforces brand identity, values, and positioning in the minds of the audience.

- **Cross-Channel Integration:** IMC integrates storytelling seamlessly across channels, creating a cohesive narrative journey for the audience. For example, a brand story introduced through a video campaign on social media may be reinforced through blog posts, email newsletters, and in-store promotions.

- **Omni-Channel Experience:** IMC strives to deliver an omni-channel experience where the audience can engage with the brand seamlessly across multiple touchpoints. Consistent storytelling enhances the omni-channel experience, driving engagement and conversion.

3. **Strategies for Aligning Narratives Across Channels:**

- **Message Mapping:** Develop a message map that outlines key storytelling messages, themes, and narratives for each channel. Ensure that messages are aligned with the overall brand story and objectives.

- **Content Repurposing:** Repurpose storytelling content across different channels while customizing it to fit the channel's format, audience expectations, and engagement metrics. For example, a long-form blog post can be repurposed into shorter social media posts, infographics, or videos.

- **Cross-Promotion:** Leverage cross-promotion strategies to amplify storytelling messages across channels. For instance, promote a social media campaign through email newsletters, website banners, and influencer partnerships to reach a wider audience.

- Data and Analytics: Use data analytics and insights to track audience engagement, sentiment, and behavior across channels. Analyze performance metrics to optimize storytelling strategies, content distribution, and channel allocation.

- Collaboration and Coordination: Foster collaboration and coordination among marketing teams, creative teams, content creators, and channel managers to ensure alignment and consistency in storytelling efforts.

- Feedback Loop: Establish a feedback loop to gather insights and feedback from the audience regarding their perception of the brand's storytelling across channels. Use feedback to refine and improve storytelling strategies over time.

4. Benefits of Integrated Marketing Communications for Storytelling:

- **Unified Brand Identity:** IMC ensures a unified and consistent brand identity across channels, enhancing brand recognition, recall, and trust among the audience.

- **Increased Engagement:** Integrated storytelling encourages audience engagement and interaction across multiple touchpoints, leading to deeper connections and brand loyalty.

- **Efficient Resource Allocation:** IMC optimizes resource allocation by focusing efforts and investments on channels that deliver the most impact and ROI for storytelling initiatives.

- **Measurable Results:** IMC allows for the measurement and evaluation of storytelling effectiveness across channels, enabling data-driven decision-making and continuous improvement.

- **Adaptability and Agility:** IMC enables brands to adapt storytelling strategies and messages based on real-time feedback, market trends, and audience preferences, ensuring relevance and agility in communication.

In summary, Integrated Marketing Communications plays a vital role in aligning narratives across channels, ensuring consistency, synergy, and effectiveness in storytelling efforts. By embracing IMC strategies, brands can deliver cohesive and impactful storytelling experiences that resonate with the audience, drive engagement, and achieve marketing objectives seamlessly across diverse communication channels.

- Storytelling in Social Media: Leveraging Visual and Interactive Elements

Storytelling in social media is a dynamic and engaging way to connect with audiences, leveraging visual and interactive elements to create compelling narratives. Social media platforms provide unique opportunities to share stories, evoke emotions, and drive engagement through multimedia content, interactive features, and real-time interactions. Let's comprehensively discuss the strategies and techniques for leveraging visual and interactive elements in storytelling on social media:

1. **Visual Storytelling Strategies:**

   - **High-Quality Imagery:** Use high-quality images and graphics that capture attention, evoke emotions, and align with your brand's visual identity. Visuals should be compelling, relevant, and optimized for each social media platform's specifications.

   - **Videos and Animations:** Incorporate videos, animations, and motion graphics to bring stories to life and create immersive storytelling experiences. Use storytelling techniques such as narrative arcs, character development, and emotional cues in video content.

   - **Infographics and Data Visualizations:** Present complex information, statistics, or processes in visually engaging formats such as infographics and data visualizations. Visual storytelling simplifies concepts, enhances understanding, and encourages sharing.

   - User-Generated Content: Encourage users to create and share user-generated content related to your brand or story. User-generated content adds authenticity, diversity, and social proof to storytelling efforts.

2. **Interactive Storytelling Techniques:**

   - Polls and Surveys: Use polls, surveys, and quizzes to engage audiences and gather feedback. Interactive polls can be used to crowdsource opinions, preferences, or ideas related to your story or brand.

   - Interactive Videos: Create interactive videos that allow viewers to make choices or explore different story paths. Interactive storytelling engages audiences actively, increasing time spent and emotional investment.

   - Live Streaming: Use live streaming features on social media platforms to conduct live storytelling sessions, Q&A sessions, behind-the-scenes tours, product demonstrations, or events. Live streaming fosters real-time interaction and engagement.

- Interactive Stories and Posts: Utilize interactive features such as Instagram Stories' polls, quizzes, and sliders, or Facebook's interactive posts to encourage audience participation and feedback. Interactive stories increase engagement and interaction rates.

3. **Storytelling Best Practices on Social Media:**

- Know Your Audience: Understand your audience's preferences, behaviors, and interests to tailor storytelling content that resonates with them. Use audience insights, analytics, and feedback to inform storytelling strategies.

- Consistent Brand Voice: Maintain a consistent brand voice, tone, and style across all storytelling content on social media. Consistency builds brand recognition, trust, and credibility.

- Emotional Appeal: Evoke emotions such as joy, curiosity, empathy, or inspiration through storytelling. Emotional storytelling creates memorable experiences and encourages sharing and engagement.

- **Storytelling Series:** Create storytelling series or campaigns that unfold over time, keeping audiences engaged and invested in the narrative. Series format builds anticipation, continuity, and storytelling depth.

- **Call to Action:** Include clear and compelling calls to action (CTAs) in storytelling content to guide audience behavior, whether it's to like, share, comment, follow, visit a website, or participate in a campaign.

4. **Optimizing Visual and Interactive Content:**

- **Platform-Specific Optimization:** Customize visual and interactive content for each social media platform's audience, format, and best practices. Optimize content for mobile devices, considering screen sizes and user interaction patterns.

- **Story Highlights and Archives:** Use story highlights, archives, or pinned posts to showcase evergreen storytelling content and keep it accessible to new and returning audiences.

- **Analytics and Insights:** Monitor social media analytics, engagement metrics, and audience feedback to evaluate the performance of visual and interactive storytelling content. Use insights to iterate, improve, and refine storytelling strategies over time.

- **Testing and Experimentation:** Experiment with different visual formats, interactive features, storytelling styles, and content lengths to discover what resonates best with your audience. A/B testing and experimentation help optimize storytelling effectiveness.

5. **Examples of Successful Visual and Interactive Storytelling on Social Media:**

- **Interactive Contests:** Run interactive contests or challenges that encourage user participation, creativity, and engagement. For example, user-generated content contests with voting mechanisms.

- **360-Degree Videos:** Use 360-degree videos to provide immersive storytelling experiences, allowing viewers to explore environments, events, or narratives from different perspectives.

- **Augmented Reality (AR) Filters:** Develop AR filters or lenses that align with your storytelling theme or brand message. AR filters enhance engagement and user interaction.

- **Storytelling Campaigns:** Launch storytelling campaigns that unfold over time, leveraging sequential storytelling, cliffhangers, and user participation. For example, episodic content releases with interactive elements.

- **Behind-the-Scenes Content:** Share behind-the-scenes content, bloopers, or exclusive insights through visual and interactive storytelling. Behind-the-scenes content humanizes your brand and fosters authenticity.

In conclusion, visual and interactive elements play a crucial role in elevating storytelling on social media, creating immersive experiences, and driving audience engagement. By leveraging high-quality imagery, videos, animations, interactive features, and storytelling best practices, brands can captivate audiences, foster emotional connections, and achieve marketing objectives effectively on social media platforms.

- Omnichannel Storytelling: Creating Seamless Experiences Across Touchpoints

Omnichannel storytelling is a strategic approach that focuses on creating seamless and cohesive narrative experiences across multiple touchpoints and channels. It aims to deliver a unified brand message, consistent storytelling themes, and personalized interactions to engage audiences at every stage of their journey. Let's comprehensively discuss the concept of omnichannel storytelling and how to create seamless experiences across touchpoints:

1. Understanding Omnichannel Storytelling:

   - Holistic Customer Journey: Omnichannel storytelling views the customer journey as a holistic experience that spans various touchpoints, both online and offline. It recognizes that customers interact with brands through multiple channels, devices, and platforms.

   - Consistency and Continuity: Omnichannel storytelling emphasizes consistency and continuity in brand messaging, storytelling themes, visuals, and tone across all touchpoints. It ensures that customers receive a unified brand experience regardless of the channel or device they use.

   - Personalization: Omnichannel storytelling leverages data and insights to personalize storytelling content, messages, and interactions based on customer preferences, behavior, and journey stage. Personalization enhances relevance, engagement, and conversion.

- **Seamless Integration:** Omnichannel storytelling integrates storytelling seamlessly across digital channels (e.g., website, social media, email, mobile apps) and physical touchpoints (e.g., stores, events, customer service) to create a seamless and immersive brand experience.

- **Optimized Customer Experience:** The goal of omnichannel storytelling is to optimize the customer experience by removing friction, providing convenience, and delivering value at every touchpoint. It aims to engage, delight, and retain customers through compelling storytelling.

2. **Key Elements of Omnichannel Storytelling:**

- **Unified Brand Story:** Omnichannel storytelling starts with a unified brand story, core messaging, values, and narrative themes that resonate with the target audience. The brand story serves as the foundation for storytelling across touchpoints.

- **Customer Segmentation:** Segment customers based on demographics, behavior, preferences, and journey stage to tailor storytelling content and messages for different audience segments. Personalized storytelling enhances relevance and engagement.

- Channel Integration: Integrate storytelling seamlessly across digital channels (e.g., website, social media, email, mobile apps) and physical channels (e.g., stores, events, customer service) to ensure a consistent and cohesive brand experience.

- Data and Insights: Use data analytics, customer feedback, and journey mapping to gain insights into customer interactions, preferences, pain points, and opportunities for storytelling optimization. Data-driven storytelling enhances effectiveness and ROI.

- Cross-Channel Coordination: Coordinate marketing, creative, and customer service teams to ensure alignment and consistency in storytelling efforts across channels. Cross-channel coordination enhances messaging clarity and brand perception.

3. **Strategies for Creating Seamless Experiences Across Touchpoints:**

 - Omni-Channel Content Strategy: Develop an omnichannel content strategy that aligns storytelling themes, formats, and messages with each touchpoint's strengths and audience expectations. Adapt storytelling content for different channels while maintaining consistency.

 - Cross-Channel Promotion: Promote storytelling content and campaigns across multiple touchpoints to reach a wider audience and reinforce messaging. For example, use social media to promote blog posts, videos, or events hosted on your website.

 - Interactive Touchpoints: Incorporate interactive elements, such as quizzes, polls, surveys, or interactive videos, across touchpoints to engage audiences actively and gather insights. Interactive storytelling enhances participation and audience interaction.

 - Seamless Transitions: Ensure seamless transitions and continuity in storytelling narratives as customers move across touchpoints. For example, a customer who discovers a product through social media should experience a consistent narrative when visiting the website or physical store.

   - Personalized Recommendations: Use data-driven personalization to deliver relevant and timely storytelling content, product recommendations, or offers based on customer behavior, preferences, and past interactions. Personalized storytelling enhances relevance and conversion rates.

   - Feedback Loop: Establish a feedback loop to gather customer feedback, sentiment, and insights across touchpoints. Use feedback to iterate, optimize, and refine storytelling strategies, content, and experiences over time.

4. **Benefits of Omnichannel Storytelling:**

   - Enhanced Customer Experience: Omnichannel storytelling enhances the customer experience by providing a seamless, consistent, and personalized brand experience across touchpoints. It reduces friction and increases engagement and satisfaction.

- Improved Brand Perception: Consistent storytelling across channels builds brand recognition, trust, and loyalty. It reinforces brand values, messaging, and positioning in the minds of customers, leading to positive brand perception.

- Increased Engagement and Conversions: Omnichannel storytelling increases engagement, interactions, and conversions by delivering relevant, timely, and compelling storytelling content at every touchpoint. It encourages customers to take desired actions and move along the customer journey.

- Data-Driven Optimization: Omnichannel storytelling allows for data-driven optimization of storytelling strategies, content, and experiences based on real-time insights, customer feedback, and performance metrics. It enables continuous improvement and agility in storytelling efforts.

5. Examples of Successful Omnichannel Storytelling:

- **Nike:** Nike's omnichannel storytelling seamlessly integrates storytelling narratives across its website, social media channels, mobile apps, retail stores, and events. The brand's storytelling focuses on empowering athletes, promoting inclusivity, and showcasing product innovation.

- **Starbucks:** Starbucks uses omnichannel storytelling to create a cohesive brand experience across its mobile app, website, social media, loyalty program, and in-store interactions. The brand's storytelling emphasizes community, sustainability, and personalized coffee experiences.

- **Apple:** Apple's omnichannel storytelling approach unifies brand messaging, product launches, and customer support across its website, retail stores, social media, and advertising campaigns. The brand's storytelling highlights innovation, creativity, and user experience.

In summary, omnichannel storytelling is essential for creating seamless and immersive brand experiences across touchpoints. By leveraging unified brand storytelling, personalized messaging, cross-channel integration, data-driven optimization, and coordinated efforts, brands can engage audiences effectively, drive loyalty, and achieve marketing objectives seamlessly across digital and physical channels.

CHAPTER 5: MEASURING SUCCESS: METRICS AND ANALYSIS FOR STORYTELLING IMPACT

In Chapter 5 of "Strategic Storytelling: Crafting Narratives for Marketing Success," titled "Measuring Success: Metrics and Analysis for Storytelling Impact," we delve into the critical aspect of evaluating the effectiveness and impact of storytelling strategies. As storytellers, marketers, and brand strategists, understanding how to measure success, analyze data, and derive actionable insights is paramount in refining storytelling approaches, optimizing campaigns, and achieving tangible results.

This chapter serves as a guide to navigating the realm of storytelling metrics, analytics, and performance measurement techniques. We explore the key metrics, KPIs (Key Performance Indicators), and tools used to assess storytelling impact across various channels, audience segments, and campaign objectives. From engagement rates and conversions to sentiment analysis and attribution modeling, we uncover the methodologies and best practices for quantifying storytelling impact and driving continuous improvement.

Join me as we embark on a journey of measurement and analysis, unlocking the power of data-driven storytelling, and leveraging insights to enhance storytelling strategies, resonate with audiences, and drive meaningful business outcomes. Whether you're a seasoned marketer seeking to optimize storytelling ROI or a budding storyteller aiming to understand the impact of your narratives, this chapter equips you with the knowledge and tools to measure success and elevate your storytelling prowess.

- Key Performance Indicators (KPIs) for Storytelling: Metrics That Matter

Key Performance Indicators (KPIs) for storytelling are metrics used to assess the effectiveness, impact, and success of storytelling initiatives across various channels, campaigns, and audience segments. These KPIs provide valuable insights into how storytelling efforts are performing, how audiences are engaging with content, and how storytelling contributes to business objectives. Let's comprehensively discuss the key KPIs for storytelling and why they matter:

1. **Engagement Metrics:**

   - **Page Views:** Measure the number of views or visits to storytelling content, such as blog posts, articles, videos, or landing pages. Page views indicate initial interest and reach.

- **Time Spent:** Evaluate the average time spent by users engaging with storytelling content. Longer time spent suggests deeper engagement and interest in the narrative.

- **Bounce Rate:** Assess the bounce rate, which is the percentage of visitors who leave a storytelling page without further interaction. A lower bounce rate indicates higher engagement and content relevance.

2. **Audience Interaction and Participation:**

- **Comments and Feedback:** Track the number of comments, feedback, and interactions received on storytelling content. Audience comments provide qualitative insights into sentiment, reactions, and engagement levels.

- **Shares and Social Engagement:** Measure the number of shares, likes, retweets, and social media interactions generated by storytelling content. Social engagement metrics reflect audience advocacy and amplification of the narrative.

- **User-Generated Content:** Monitor the creation and sharing of user-generated content related to storytelling campaigns or themes. User-generated content indicates audience involvement and brand affinity.

3. **Conversion Metrics:**

- **Click-Through Rate (CTR):** Evaluate the CTR of storytelling elements, such as calls to action (CTAs), links, or interactive elements. A higher CTR indicates effective storytelling in driving user actions.

- **Conversion Rate:** Measure the conversion rate, which is the percentage of users who take desired actions, such as signing up, making a purchase, or downloading content, after engaging with storytelling content.

- **Attribution Modeling:** Use attribution models to track and attribute conversions to storytelling touchpoints along the customer journey. Attribution modeling helps understand the impact of storytelling on conversion paths and outcomes.

4. **Brand Perception and Sentiment:**

- **Sentiment Analysis:** Analyze sentiment data from audience comments, reviews, and social media mentions related to storytelling content. Sentiment analysis provides insights into how audiences perceive and respond to the narrative.

- **Brand Mentions:** Monitor brand mentions, hashtags, and conversations related to storytelling campaigns or themes across social media platforms. Positive brand mentions indicate brand affinity and storytelling resonance.

5. **Audience Segmentation and Behavior:**

- **Demographics:** Segment audience engagement metrics by demographics, such as age, gender, location, interests, or behavior. Demographic segmentation provides insights into audience preferences and content relevance.

- **Behavioral Metrics:** Analyze audience behavior metrics, such as click patterns, content consumption paths, and interaction sequences. Behavioral metrics reveal how audiences engage with storytelling content and navigate through narratives.

6. Content Performance and Optimization:

- **Content Reach:** Measure the reach and visibility of storytelling content across channels and platforms. Assess reach metrics, such as impressions, reach, and share of voice, to understand content distribution and amplification.

- **Content Performance:** Evaluate the performance of different storytelling formats, topics, and themes based on engagement, conversion, and audience feedback. Use performance data to optimize content strategy and storytelling approaches.

7. Return on Investment (ROI) and Business Impact:

- **Cost per Acquisition (CPA):** Calculate the cost per acquisition of customers or leads attributed to storytelling efforts. CPA helps assess the efficiency and cost-effectiveness of storytelling campaigns.

- **Revenue Attribution:** Attribute revenue or business outcomes, such as sales, subscriptions, or brand loyalty, to storytelling touchpoints. Revenue attribution measures the direct impact of storytelling on business results.

   - **ROI Analysis:** Conduct ROI analysis to evaluate the return on investment from storytelling initiatives. ROI analysis considers costs, revenues, and benefits derived from storytelling efforts.

8. **Long-Term Impact and Loyalty:**

   - **Customer Lifetime Value (CLV):** Assess the customer lifetime value generated from storytelling-engaged customers. CLV measures the long-term impact of storytelling on customer loyalty, repeat purchases, and lifetime value.

   - **Retention Rate:** Monitor customer retention rates among storytelling-engaged audiences compared to non-engaged segments. Higher retention rates indicate storytelling effectiveness in building customer loyalty.

Why These KPIs Matter:

- Performance Evaluation: KPIs provide a quantitative basis for evaluating the performance and impact of storytelling initiatives. They help assess what's working, what's not, and where improvements are needed.

- Data-Driven Decisions: KPIs enable data-driven decision-making by providing actionable insights into audience behavior, content performance, and campaign effectiveness. They guide optimization strategies and resource allocation.

- Alignment with Objectives: KPIs align storytelling efforts with business objectives, marketing goals, and audience expectations. They measure progress toward key outcomes and ROI.

- Continuous Improvement: KPIs support continuous improvement and optimization of storytelling strategies, content formats, messaging, and audience targeting. They facilitate learning, experimentation, and adaptation based on performance data.

- **Demonstrating Impact:** KPIs help demonstrate the impact of storytelling on business results, customer engagement, brand perception and revenue generation. They communicate storytelling ROI and value to stakeholders.

In conclusion, the key performance indicators (KPIs) for storytelling play a crucial role in measuring success, evaluating impact, and optimizing storytelling strategies. By tracking engagement metrics, audience interaction, conversion rates, brand sentiment, audience segmentation, content performance, ROI, and long-term impact, marketers can gain valuable insights, make informed decisions, and drive continuous improvement in storytelling effectiveness and business outcomes.

- Data Analytics and Storytelling: Using Insights to Refine Narrative Strategies

Data analytics plays a pivotal role in refining narrative strategies by providing actionable insights into audience behavior, content performance, and campaign effectiveness. The integration of data analytics with storytelling enables marketers and content creators to make data-driven decisions, optimize storytelling approaches, and enhance engagement with target audiences. Let's comprehensively discuss how data analytics can be used to refine narrative strategies:

1. **Audience Insights and Segmentation:**

   - **Demographic Data**: Utilize demographic data such as age, gender, location, income, and education level to segment audiences and tailor storytelling content to specific demographic groups. Understanding audience demographics helps in crafting relevant and personalized narratives.

- **Behavioral Data:** Analyze behavioral data including website visits, content consumption patterns, click-through rates, time spent on pages, and social media interactions. Behavioral insights reveal how audiences engage with storytelling content and what types of narratives resonate most.

- **Audience Personas:** Develop detailed audience personas based on data analytics to create targeted storytelling strategies. Personas incorporate audience characteristics, preferences, pain points, motivations, and journey stages, guiding the creation of compelling narratives.

- **Sentiment Analysis:** Use sentiment analysis tools to analyze audience sentiment, reactions, and emotions expressed in comments, reviews, and social media interactions. Sentiment analysis helps gauge audience perception and sentiment towards storytelling content and brand messaging.

2. **Content Performance Analysis:**

  - **Engagement Metrics:** Track engagement metrics such as page views, time spent on page, bounce rate, social shares, likes, comments, and click-through rates. Engagement metrics indicate how effectively storytelling content captures audience attention, generates interactions, and encourages further exploration.

  - **Conversion Metrics:** Evaluate conversion metrics including conversion rates, lead generation, form submissions, downloads, sign-ups, and purchases attributed to storytelling efforts. Conversion metrics measure the impact of storytelling on driving desired actions and achieving business objectives.

  - **Content A/B Testing:** Conduct A/B testing experiments to compare different storytelling formats, headlines, visuals, calls to action (CTAs), and content variations. A/B testing helps identify high-performing elements and optimize storytelling content for maximum impact.

- **Funnel Analysis:** Analyze the customer journey and conversion funnel to identify bottlenecks, drop-off points, and areas for improvement in storytelling strategies. Funnel analysis uncovers insights into how storytelling influences customer decision-making and behavior at each stage of the journey.

3. **Channel Performance and Optimization:**

- **Multi-Channel Attribution:** Use multi-channel attribution models to attribute conversions and engagement metrics to specific storytelling touchpoints across channels. Multi-channel attribution provides insights into the effectiveness of different channels in driving storytelling impact and customer actions.

- **Channel Comparison:** Compare the performance of storytelling content across various channels, including social media platforms, websites, email campaigns, paid advertising, and offline channels. Channel comparison helps allocate resources effectively and prioritize high-performing channels.

- **Optimization Strategies:** Implement optimization strategies based on data analytics findings, such as refining content distribution strategies, adjusting messaging based on channel preferences, optimizing ad targeting and placement, and reallocating budget towards top-performing channels.

4. **Audience Feedback and Iteration:**

   - **Surveys and Feedback:** Collect audience feedback through surveys, polls, focus groups, and customer interviews to gather qualitative insights into storytelling preferences, perceptions, and areas for improvement. Audience feedback guides iterative refinement of narrative strategies.

   - **Iterative Content Creation:** Adopt an iterative content creation approach based on data-driven feedback and performance analysis. Continuously iterate and refine storytelling content, messaging, formats, and delivery methods to align with audience expectations and preferences.

- **Agile Experimentation:** Embrace agile experimentation and rapid testing methodologies to test hypotheses, explore new storytelling ideas, and iterate quickly based on data insights. Agile experimentation fosters innovation, learning, and optimization in narrative strategies.

5. Predictive Analytics and Future Planning:

- **Predictive Modeling:** Leverage predictive analytics and machine learning algorithms to forecast audience behavior, content performance trends, and campaign outcomes. Predictive modeling helps in strategic decision-making, resource allocation, and future planning for storytelling initiatives.

- **Trend Analysis:** Analyze industry trends, market dynamics, competitor strategies, and cultural shifts using data analytics to inform storytelling strategies. Trend analysis enables proactive adaptation, relevance, and agility in narrative planning.

- **Long-term Strategy Alignment:** Align data analytics findings with long-term storytelling strategies, brand narratives, and business goals. Use data-driven insights to inform storytelling roadmaps, content calendars, and messaging frameworks for sustained impact and relevance.

In conclusion, data analytics serves as a powerful tool for refining narrative strategies by providing actionable insights into audience behavior, content performance, channel effectiveness, audience feedback, and predictive trends. By leveraging data analytics, marketers and content creators can optimize storytelling approaches, enhance audience engagement, drive conversions, and achieve business objectives effectively. Data-driven storytelling enables continuous learning, adaptation, and innovation in crafting compelling narratives that resonate with target audiences and drive meaningful impact.

- ROI of Storytelling: Evaluating the Business Impact of Narrative-driven Marketing

The Return on Investment (ROI) of storytelling refers to the assessment of the business impact and financial returns generated by narrative-driven marketing initiatives. Evaluating the ROI of storytelling involves measuring the effectiveness, efficiency, and contribution of storytelling efforts to achieving business objectives, driving revenue, and creating tangible value for the organization. Let's comprehensively discuss the ROI of storytelling and how to evaluate the business impact of narrative-driven marketing:

1. **Defining ROI in Storytelling:**

   - **Financial Impact:** ROI in storytelling quantifies the financial impact of storytelling initiatives, campaigns, or content creation efforts. It assesses the return generated relative to the investment made in storytelling activities, resources, and assets.

- **Business Value:** ROI measures the business value derived from storytelling, including increased brand awareness, customer engagement, lead generation, conversion rates, sales revenue, customer retention, and loyalty.

- **Long-term Impact:** ROI analysis considers both short-term and long-term impact, taking into account the sustained benefits, competitive advantage, and strategic value of storytelling investments over time.

2. **Key Components of ROI Analysis in Storytelling:**

- **Cost Analysis:** Calculate the total cost incurred in developing and executing storytelling initiatives, including content creation costs, marketing expenses, personnel salaries, technology investments, and campaign budgets.

- **Revenue Generation:** Measure the revenue generated directly attributed to storytelling efforts, such as sales revenue from storytelling-driven campaigns, product launches, promotions, or customer acquisition initiatives.

- **Attribution Modeling:** Use attribution models to attribute revenue, conversions, and business outcomes to specific storytelling touchpoints, channels, or campaigns along the customer journey. Attribution modeling helps in assigning credit and understanding the impact of storytelling on revenue generation.

3. **Metrics for ROI Evaluation in Storytelling:**

- Conversion Rates: Evaluate conversion rates associated with storytelling-driven campaigns, content, or customer interactions. Measure the percentage of leads, prospects, or website visitors who take desired actions, such as making a purchase, signing up, or downloading content.

- **Customer Acquisition Cost (CAC):** Calculate the cost per customer acquisition attributed to storytelling efforts. CAC compares the total cost of acquiring customers with the number of customers acquired, providing insights into the efficiency of storytelling in acquiring new customers.

- **Customer Lifetime Value (CLV):** Assess the customer lifetime value generated from storytelling-engaged customers over their entire relationship with the brand. CLV measures the long-term revenue potential and profitability of storytelling-driven customer relationships.

- **Engagement Metrics:** Track engagement metrics, such as time spent on page, bounce rate, social shares, comments, and click-through rates, to assess audience engagement with storytelling content and its impact on brand interactions.

- **Brand Perception:** Conduct brand perception surveys, sentiment analysis, and brand health metrics to measure changes in audience perception, sentiment, awareness, loyalty, and advocacy influenced by storytelling efforts.

- **Social Impact:** Evaluate social impact metrics, including social media reach, engagement, mentions, sentiment, and brand sentiment scores, to gauge storytelling's influence on social conversations, brand visibility, and community engagement.

4. **ROI Calculation Formula:**

   - ROI (%) = (Net Profit / Total Investment) x 100

   - Net Profit = Revenue Generated - Total Cost

   - Total Investment = Cost of Storytelling Initiatives + Marketing Expenses

5. **Benefits of Evaluating ROI in Storytelling:**

   - **Data-Driven Decision Making:** ROI analysis provides data-driven insights that inform strategic decision-making, resource allocation, and investment prioritization in storytelling initiatives.

   - **Optimization and Efficiency:** By measuring ROI, organizations can identify high-performing storytelling strategies, channels, content types, and campaigns, allowing them to optimize resources, improve efficiency, and maximize returns.

  - Alignment with Business Goals: ROI evaluation ensures that storytelling efforts align with business goals, marketing objectives, and key performance indicators (KPIs), demonstrating the value and impact of storytelling on achieving desired outcomes.

  - Demonstrating Value: ROI analysis helps in demonstrating the value of storytelling to stakeholders, executives, and investors by showcasing tangible results, revenue contributions, cost efficiencies, and ROI metrics.

  - Continuous Improvement: Continuous ROI evaluation enables continuous improvement, iteration, and innovation in storytelling strategies, content creation, messaging, and audience targeting to enhance business impact and ROI over time.

6. **Challenges and Considerations:**

  - Attribution Complexity: Attribution of revenue and business outcomes to storytelling efforts can be complex due to multi-touchpoint customer journeys, cross-channel interactions, and attribution challenges. Implementing robust attribution models and data analytics tools can help overcome attribution complexities.

- **Long-term Impact:** Evaluating the long-term impact of storytelling, such as brand loyalty, customer lifetime value, and competitive differentiation, requires ongoing tracking, analysis, and measurement beyond immediate ROI metrics.

- **Data Integration:** Integrating data from multiple sources, systems, and platforms for ROI analysis requires data integration strategies, data governance, and collaboration across departments, teams, and stakeholders.

In conclusion, evaluating the ROI of storytelling is essential for assessing the business impact, financial returns, and value generated by narrative-driven marketing initiatives. By analyzing key metrics, conducting cost-benefit analysis, calculating ROI, and considering long-term impact, organizations can measure the effectiveness of storytelling, make data-driven decisions, optimize strategies, and demonstrate the value of storytelling in achieving business objectives and driving revenue growth.

CONCLUSION

In conclusion, "Strategic Storytelling: Crafting Narratives for Marketing Success" encapsulates the transformative power of storytelling in the realm of modern marketing. Through the chapters of this book, we've explored the intricate art of crafting compelling narratives that resonate with audiences, drive engagement, and ultimately contribute to business success.

From understanding the psychology of storytelling and adapting to digital platforms to developing brand narratives and leveraging emotional engagement, each chapter has provided invaluable insights and practical strategies for harnessing the full potential of storytelling in marketing endeavors.

We've delved into the nuances of storytelling metrics, analyzed the impact of narratives across channels, and discussed the importance of measuring ROI to demonstrate the tangible value of storytelling initiatives. By aligning storytelling with business goals, optimizing content strategies, and leveraging data analytics, organizations can create meaningful connections with their audiences, foster brand loyalty, and achieve measurable results.

As we navigate the ever-evolving landscape of marketing, one thing remains constant: the timeless allure of storytelling. It is not merely about conveying information but about sparking emotions, fostering connections, and shaping perceptions. "Strategic Storytelling" serves as a guide, empowering marketers, entrepreneurs, and storytellers alike to harness the narrative magic and unlock the doors to marketing success.

May the insights gleaned from these pages inspire you to craft narratives that captivate, resonate, and drive impactful outcomes. Let your stories be the guiding light that illuminates the path to deeper engagement, stronger brand affinity, and enduring success in the dynamic world of marketing.

Remember, the journey of strategic storytelling is not just about crafting narratives—it's about creating experiences, forging connections, and leaving a lasting impression. Here's to the power of storytelling and its endless possibilities in shaping the future of marketing excellence.

www.ingramcontent.com/pod-product-compliance
Lightning Source LLC
Chambersburg PA
CBHW070152230526
45471CB00002B/626